CURIO NO. 2

HOW TO TALK LIKE YOU KNOW WHAT YOU'RE TALKING ABOUT

MASTER THE ART OF CONVERSATION

MATTHEW DOUCET

CIDER MILL PRESS

BOOK
PUBLISHERS
KENNEBUNKPORT, MAINE

13-Digit ISBN: 978-1-60433-862-1
10-Digit ISBN: 1-60433-862-8

This book may be ordered by mail from the publisher. Please include $5.99 for postage and handling. Please support your local bookseller first!

Books published by Cider Mill Press Book Publishers are available at special discounts for bulk purchases in the United States by corporations, institutions, and other organizations. For more information, please contact the publisher.

Cider Mill Press Book Publishers
"Where good books are ready for press"
PO Box 454
12 Spring Street
Kennebunkport, Maine 04046
Visit us online!
www.cidermillpress.com

Typography: Rival

Printed in China
1 2 3 4 5 6 7 8 9 0
First Edition

CONTENTS

Introduction   5

Coda   8

Genghis Khan   11

Thomas Pynchon   15

Giants of Jazz   18

The Strange Beliefs of Advanced Societies   21

Odd Jobs   25

Big Sur   29

Gerrymandering   32

The Source   35

Jane Jacobs   38

Brian Eno   44

Banana Extinction   47

Grand Central Terminal   50

The Bicameral Mind   55

Quincy Jones   59

Museum of Broken Relationships   64

Magic Mushrooms   67

Gary Ridgway   70

Unknown Legends   74

Instant Erudition   77

John McPhee   81

Robert Oppenheimer	86
On Writing	90
Elliott Smith	95
Accidental Discoveries	98
The Boxer Rebellion	102
Memory	106
Fiona Apple	111
Joan of Arc	115
Remain in Light	121
Ranked-Choice Voting	125
A League of Their Own	130
Beds Made by the CIA	135
Relativity	140
The Causes of World War I	143
Marshall McLuhan	149
Surfing	153
Color	158
Josephine Baker	162
Way of the Pilgrim	165
Virginia Woolf	170
Hells Angels	175
Stevie Wonder	179
Where Is My Mind?	182
Richard Nixon: Liberal Messiah	187

INTRODUCTION

While it may appear that a number of adolescent motivations—a desire for admiration, a fear of being ignored, an aversion to structure, boredom, and hard work—are guiding this book, it is in actuality an acknowledgment of an often overlooked truth: that pretension and affectation have the ability to construct a pathway to someplace higher (see: Bowie, David; and Dylan, Bob).

Sure, this array of topics and facts will enable you to take over a corner at a party and dazzle anyone who happens by. And yes, they'll prevent you from being cursed with the contemporary affliction that David Byrne succinctly diagnosed in "Psycho Killer": "You're talking a lot, but you're not saying anything."

But the true aim of this book is to cultivate a belief in the power of a chance encounter with a seemingly trivial piece of information. To make palpable the truth residing in this insight from James Baldwin: "The world changes according to the way people see it, and if you alter, even by a millimeter, the way a person looks or people look at reality, then you can change it."

What has been gathered in these pages is far more than a prop to be used in some parlor trick. It instead becomes a means of developing the eyes, ears, and mind-set required to distinguish signal from noise and forge connections between seemingly disparate subjects—abilities that are indispensable in a world where information is increasingly used to silence and obfuscate, and interpersonal exchange is defined and impoverished by the internet and its associated technologies.

Exposure to such an illuminating array of material, and the intoxicating effects of the attention stemming from the deployment of it, can foster a tendency to become insufferable. So, never forget: the information you offer up and the people you share it with are of greater interest than you. Don't hesitate to relay those things that have transformed your view of the world, but make sure you leave space for others to respond in kind.

CODA

Travel, narcotics, and the emotional turbulence associated with a creative life have combined to make popular music a strangely hazardous and tragic land. Even amongst all that wreckage, a few deaths stand out.

OTIS BLUE

Most people know that Otis Redding died in a plane crash, but it's actually far more heartbreaking than that. Redding was on a plane that crashed into a lake, and he survived the impact. Unfortunately, Redding was either knocked unconscious or unable to swim, and he drowned.

THE DEMISE OF T. REX: A GREEK TRAGEDY

Marc Bolan, the lead singer of T. Rex, was killed just before his 30th birthday when a car he was a passenger in got into an accident. Bolan never learned to drive because he feared dying prematurely in an automobile accident.

A SERIES OF UNFORTUNATE EVENTS

Nico, famous for her haunting vocals on The Velvet Underground's influential first album, died after a heart attack caused her to fall from the bicycle she was riding. She hit her head, and may have survived, but the hospital misdiagnosed both the heart attack and head injury, believing that she was only suffering from heat exhaustion.

THAT'S A NIGHTMARE

Mikey Welsh, the one-time bassist for Weezer, died from a drug overdose in 2011. Unfortunately, there's nothing particularly strange about that in the music world. The weirdness lies in a Twitter post made by Welsh 12 days before his death, in which he predicted where and when his death would take place.

GENGHIS KHAN

He and his Mongol hordes are notorious for laying waste to everything set before them, but Khan's talents weren't restricted to destruction.

A VAST DOMINION

Khan is related to 0.5 percent (16 million) of the current global male population. This lineage has been traced through a genetic mutation that Khan possessed—and which his wide-spanning empire allowed to proliferate.

DESOLATION ROW

Legend has it that Khan's funeral escort executed everyone in their path so that the location of his grave would remain secret and his body undisturbed.

WE'VE GOT TO LIVE TOGETHER

While he is famous for leveling entire cities, Khan's first major step toward becoming a massive historical personage was uniting the nomadic, insular clans that occupied the plains of Mongolia. Khan's considerable charisma and revolutionary leadership style—which included rewarding loyalty and merit rather than noble bloodlines—were the keys to winning the fealty of these disparate tribes.

ALL MY FRIENDS

Khan, who studied Islam, Buddhism, Taoism, and Christianity, remains light-years ahead of some present-day leaders in terms of religious tolerance. Though he was a follower of Mongolian shamanism, Khan included a Taoist sage in his retinue for a time and provided tax relief to a number of religious institutions. Khan also trusted individuals from other cultures to administer the cities he had taken over.

THE ULTIMATE DISCOVERY

In order to power the entire Earth on renewable energy, we would need to install solar panels on over 191,000 square miles. That seems like a considerable allotment, until one recognizes that there are currently more than 57 million square miles of open space on the planet. Even in an enterprising nation like the U.S., just 4.47 percent of the country's 3,797,000 square miles have been developed.

THOMAS PYNCHON

His famously hermetic lifestyle and a series of labyrinthine novels have always overshadowed a razor-sharp comedic wit.

YOU KNOW NOTHING OF MY WORK

Pynchon took a literature class with Vladimir Nabokov while a student at Cornell. The legendary Russian author could not recall Pynchon as an undergraduate, but Nabokov's wife, Vera, remembered Pynchon's distinctive handwriting (a mix of printing and cursive).

A SMALL, GOOD THING

Pynchon was the first one to refer to a psychiatrist with the now-ubiquitous appellation "shrink." This slangy shortening of "head shrinker" appeared in *The Crying of Lot 49.*

BLACK MATH

Pynchon's application to study mathematics as a graduate student at the University of California was rejected in 1964, one year after the publication of his debut novel, *V*. If he'd been accepted, it's safe to assume that his two greatest books, *The Crying of Lot 49* and *Gravity's Rainbow*, would never have come to pass.

GOT TO GIVE IT UP

Pynchon and Paul Thomas Anderson have more in common than *Inherent Vice*, Pynchon's '60s noir that Anderson adapted into a 2014 film. Both men burst onto the scene with a brilliant, darkly comic, and fast-paced work—*The Crying of Lot 49* for Pynchon and *Boogie Nights* for Anderson—and once they had everyone's attention, their work became increasingly idiosyncratic and byzantine, breaking completely with the approaches that provided them a platform.

GIANTS
OF JAZZ

The breadth and depth of jazz make it daunting to dive into, but if you strategically deploy these few nuggets, you'll seem like something of an aficionado.

WHAT YOU DO MATTERS

The brilliant, and notoriously eccentric, Thelonious Monk is the second most recorded jazz composer, behind only Duke Ellington. Monk wrote around 70 pieces, whereas Ellington composed more than 1,000. Other musicians like to cover Monk for his rare combination of inventiveness and accessibility, as composer and pianist Ethan Iverson pointed out: "Monk is the perfect avant-garde guy because you can dance to [his music]. Your child can sing the songs."

YOU DON'T KNOW HOW IT FEELS

Miles Davis would not shake hands before a performance, and it had nothing to do with the famously mercurial trumpeter's mood. He believed the oils from other people's palms would adversely affect the touch of his own finely attuned hands.

TAKE IT TO THE BRIDGE

Despite being widely regarded as the finest tenor saxophonist in jazz, Sonny Rollins took a hiatus in 1959 to "learn his instrument" after seeing Coleman Hawkins play. Over the course of more than two years, Rollins went out on the pedestrian walkway of New York City's Williamsburg Bridge and practiced for hours in complete anonymity. The time away paid off, resulting in a restrained, meditative sound that Rollins has wowed audiences with into the 21st century.

A LOVE SUPREME

The spiritual element in John Coltrane's late-period works has been felt by millions, but a few individuals really took it to heart, founding the Church of John Coltrane in San Francisco in 1969. Perhaps the greatest testament to the other-worldly quality of Coltrane's music is that the church continues to this day, as the Saint John Will-I-Am Coltrane African Orthodox Church.

THE STRANGE BELIEFS OF ADVANCED SOCIETIES

Certain atavisms continue to hang on in places where it seems everyone knows better.

WHITE NOISE

South Koreans almost universally believe that running an electric fan in an enclosed room poses a grave danger to whoever is in that room. The misconception is tied to a belief that by circulating stale air, a fan causes an individual to choke on the carbon dioxide that they've exhaled.

OBVIOUSLY, YOU'RE NOT A GOLFER

A number of Japanese people suffer from tetraphobia: a fear of the number 4. This is due to the word for 4 (*shi*) being the same as the word for death. Most elevators skip the fourth floor, rooms numbered 4 and 40 through 49 are typically skipped in hotels and hospitals, and giving four of something to somebody is strongly discouraged. The fear is so embedded in the culture that the Japanese camera maker Fuji jumped from the series 3 to the series 5 in its production lines.

FEAR IN A
HANDFUL OF DUST

In the United States, the individual purchase of Claritin D, an allergy relief medication, is closely monitored and restricted to 30 doses a month. This is due to the medication containing pseudoephedrine, which can be used in the production of methamphetamine. There were 3,728 deaths from methamphetamine use in 2014, which is the last year complete data was available. The Centers for Disease Control reported 36,252 firearm-related deaths in the U.S. in 2017.

RACE CAR IN THE RED

Legendary character actor Harry Dean Stanton always seemed to be in an enviable place, whether it be serving as Jack Nicholson's best man, stealing a scene in *Cool Hand Luke*, or being chosen to honor Hunter S. Thompson with a song at his funeral. But on the famously difficult shoot for *Pat Garrett and Billy the Kid*, director Sam Peckinpah threw a knife at Stanton and also drew a gun on him, both times for getting in the way and messing up a shot.

ODD JOBS

Almost everyone has had to work a job that didn't represent their true nature, even these famous figures.

HI, I'M IN DELAWARE

For a brief period in 1966, Jamaica's favorite son, Bob Marley, lived in Wilmington, Delaware, and worked as a lab assistant at DuPont and at a Chrysler assembly plant under the name Donald Marley.

WE'RE ONLY IN IT FOR THE MONEY

The notorious iconoclast Frank Zappa founded his own advertising agency in 1967 and made ads for Hagström guitars and Remington razor blades. That same year, he also scored an ad for Luden's cough drops that went on to win a Clio Award (the Academy Awards of the advertising world) for "Best Use of Sound."

ANOTHER COUNTRY

Believing he had resolved all of the issues of philosophy with his *Tractatus Logico-Philosophicus*, Ludwig Wittgenstein retreated to rural Austria to teach elementary school for six years. Inspired to work with peasants by his love of Tolstoy, Wittgenstein gave up a considerable family fortune and his academic throne to humbly devote himself to elementary education, even sleeping in the kitchen at one school. As demanding of his students as he was of himself, Wittgenstein's time teaching youths came to an abrupt end after he struck down a sickly child out of anger. Though the incident did not cost him his position in the corporal punishment–friendly era, Wittgenstein was so aghast at his behavior that he slunk back to his role as the 20th century's greatest philosopher.

THE NADIR

Reclusive author J. D. Salinger wasn't always able to avoid the spotlight. Salinger once filled the extremely gregarious role of entertainment director on a cruise ship, a Swedish luxury liner known as the HMS *Kungsholm*. The short story "Teddy," which appears in the fabled collection *Nine Stories*, is a result of Salinger's experience aboard the ship.

BIG SUR

*Let people know that it's much more than a
series of shots to throw up on Instagram.*

WE DON'T LIVE HERE ANYMORE

While the scenic area receives about the same amount of visitors as Yosemite National Park, its population is only 839. It is one of the few destinations on the West Coast that has actually seen its population decline since 2000; the stunning lack of development is likely the reason it is able to maintain its splendor and appeal generation after generation.

WHAT'S IN A NAME?

The grandeur of the mountains plunging into the sea makes the name of the region seem particularly fitting, but in fact the appellation is the result of a clunky anglicization. The region was named by the Spanish settlers in nearby Monterey, who called it *el país grande del sur*, "the big country of the south." The English-speaking settlers, needing to choose a name for their post office, christened it "Big Sur" in 1915.

THE MILLER'S TALE

The region's beauty has inspired lyrical descriptions from millions, but none can match the sentiment of this offering from longtime resident Henry Miller: "Big Sur is the California that men dreamed of years ago, this is the Pacific that Balboa looked at from the Peak of Darien, this is the face of the earth as the Creator intended it to look."

A CHANGE IS GONNA COME

The location of Esalen Institute, the famed New Age retreat, was once a dilapidated hotel. In 1960, one section of the hotel was inhabited by a Pentecostal church, a 19-year-old Joan Baez lived on the lawn, and the caretaker was a not-yet-gonzo Hunter S. Thompson, who patrolled the grounds armed with a gun.

GERRYMANDERING

*You've heard of it. You may even have a vague
sense that it refers to political maneuvering.
Here's all you need to know about this
undemocratic scourge.*

NOT JUST A CLEVER NICKNAME

The term originated in 1812, when Elbridge Gerry, the governor of Massachusetts, redrew election districts for the state senate in order to benefit his Democratic-Republican party, with one of the rejiggered districts said to resemble a salamander. While Gerry did lose his position in the election, his ploy kept the Federalists from taking the senate.

TO THE VICTORS GO THE SPOILS

The main goal of redistricting is concentrating votes in districts that an opposing candidate is already sure to win. This makes every additional vote, which is in excess of the minimum needed to win, "wasted" (i.e. win the popular vote by three million and still lose the presidency).

ACTUALLY, JUST GIVE ME POWER

While Gerry's machinations gave birth to the term, it was not the first instance of such maneuvering. An earlier attempt was spearheaded by Patrick Henry (famed for his declaration of "Give me liberty, or give me death"), who in 1788 redrew a Virginia district in an unsuccessful bid to keep future president James Madison out of the U.S. House of Representatives.

THE PRISONER'S DILEMMA

Prisoners are counted as residents of a district even though they cannot vote. This has been used to bulk up the population of the rural districts that contain large prisons, even though their population consists largely of individuals from elsewhere.

THE SOURCE

While the new will always overshadow the old in popular culture, you'd do well to keep people apprised of these overlooked influencers.

THOSE WHO CAME BEFORE ME

When Ian Curtis took his own life in 1980, the hole the charismatic singer left was more than big enough for the rest of Joy Division to fall into. But Bernard Sumner, Peter Hook, and Stephen Morris reformed as New Order and, with the help of "Blue Monday," managed to stay the course and take popular music in a new direction. The seven-minute track blends Joy Division's signature moodiness with an assault of drum machines and squelchy bits that feel better suited to the club than radio airwaves. It's an unlikely marriage, but an arrangement lifted from Klein & M.B.O.'s "Dirty Talk" (a slice of Italo disco that is as seductive as the title suggests) and the infectious, muscular bass line from Sylvester's "You Make Me Feel (Mighty Real)" hold it together.

OVER THE LINE

The famous bass line in Melle Mel's early rap classic "White Lines" was taken from Liquid

Liquid's "Cavern," which is an unbeatable choice if you want to get the party started and still receive kudos for your far-ranging taste.

AND A GOOD DAY TO YOU, SIR

The impossibly cool backing track for Ice Cube's anthem "It Was a Good Day" comes from the Isley Brothers' "Footsteps in the Dark." The inspiration is far more forlorn than Cube's victory lap, but sounds just as good on a summer evening.

TAKE WHAT YOU THINK WILL LAST

As the centerpiece of Beck's seminal *Odelay*, "Jack-Ass," is an example of a master at the height of his powers. The dreamy backing track was lifted from "It's All Over Now, Baby Blue" by the Van Morrison–backed outfit Them, a version that somehow manages to outdo Bob Dylan's massive original.

JANE JACOBS

This impassioned activist looked out her window and ended up teaching the experts how a city works.

HEAD AND HEART

After attending Columbia's School of General Studies for two years, Jacobs "became the property of Barnard College at Columbia, and once I was the property of Barnard I had to take, it seemed, what Barnard wanted me to take, not what I wanted to learn. Fortunately, my high-school marks had been so bad that Barnard decided I could not belong to it and I was therefore allowed to continue getting an education."

NEW YORK, I LOVE YOU BUT YOU'RE BRINGING ME DOWN

Jacobs was far more than a theorist, and backed up her speculations on urban life with action, and activism. She took on the improbably powerful Robert Moses (seriously, take a look at Robert Caro's *The Power Broker*—dude was the king of New York for a time) and thwarted his plans to build an expressway through Manhattan's Greenwich Village in the 1950s. Jacobs was also arrested at a public hearing for another Moses-backed roadway in 1968 and charged with inciting a riot and obstructing public administration.

I WONDER WHY PROGRESS LOOKS SO MUCH LIKE DESTRUCTION

Her landmark contributions to urban planning were fostered while she was on assignment in Philadelphia for *Architectural Forum*. Expected to produce a positive story about development in the city, Jacobs instead criticized the projects underway, calling out the lack of concern for the communities affected and disparaging the discouragement of organic communal interaction.

BRING IT ON HOME

Jacobs's writing on economics is overshadowed by her considerable contributions to urban planning, but she is equally insightful in diagnosing what is required to keep an economy from falling into decline: import replacement, the process of locally manufacturing goods that were previously purchased from somewhere else. This development fosters expansion by creating a need for goods used in the production process and possibilities for export, and also allows for the purchase of other imports that can be replaced later on. The 18th-century ascents of Boston and Philadelphia, and the more recent Brooklyn renaissance, are clear evidence of import replacement's effectiveness.

LONG, STRANGE TRIP

Owsley Stanley, who produced much of the LSD consumed on the West Coast during the explosion of the 1960s countercultural movement (and who LSD creator Albert Hoffmann said "was the only one who ever got the crystallization process right"), used some of his earnings to fund the Grateful Dead when the band was starting out. Stanley later worked as the soundman for the group, conceived their famous "Wall of Sound" public address system, and created the iconic "Steal Your Face" logo.

BRIAN ENO

This producer and musician's impeccable resume is the result of a rare combination of openness and discipline.

CAN YOU FEEL IT?

Eno, an atheist, loves gospel music. The contradiction worried him at first, as he asked himself: "Why am I so moved by a music based on something that I just don't believe in?" Ultimately, he decided that the surrender and optimism present in the music dwarfed the importance of the lyrical content.

ROAD TO NOWHERE

Eno had to be physically restrained from deleting the take of "Where the Streets Have No Name" that opens U2's *The Joshua Tree*, which he produced (along with Daniel Lanois and Steve Lillywhite). Eno believed the song that became one of the band's signature anthems was not even worthy of appearing on an album.

TOO MUCH FUN

The Velvet Underground's third album, *The Velvet Underground*, is one of Eno's favorites, providing the "moment where I realised that I could be a musician." In fact, he loved the album so much that he refused to buy it, not wanting "it to become casual for me. . . . I would only hear it at other people's places because I always wanted it to be special."

DON'T SWEAT THE TECHNIQUE

Most assume that a producer of Eno's stature has to be a technical wizard, but he spent much of his production career not even knowing the names of the knobs, buttons, and faders he was controlling on the mixing board. He understood only what they did to the sound, and whether they would bring his concept closer to fruition.

BANANA EXTINCTION

The bounty that produces their negligible price and considerable presence at every grocery store offers no hint of this fruit's precarious position.

THAT'S GROS

Due to Panama disease, a fungal pathogen that affects the roots of banana plants, the main cultivar of banana—the Gros Michel—was wiped out during the 1950s. The Gros Michel was more aromatic, more floral, fruitier, and sweeter than the Cavendish that we consume today. It was initially chosen for commercial production due to its thicker peel, which made it resistant to bruising during transport.

TIME IS A FLAT CIRCLE

New strains of Panama disease are threatening production of the Cavendish, even though it was chosen back in the '50s because it was thought to be immune.

AS I LAY DYING

Echoing the primary attitude the business community has toward global warming today, many U.S. banana executives during the 1950s were hesitant to acknowledge that there was an issue upon learning of Panama disease, and waited until the very last minute to respond.

BRAVE NEW WORLD

The considerable devastation from disease is due to the banana's lack of genetic diversity, which is required for the health and resilience of any species. Each Cavendish banana is actually an identical twin to the one that was originally cultivated, as bananas never sexually reproduce on their own.

GRAND
CENTRAL
TERMINAL

*The romantic bustle of this hub has
established it as an emblem of New York City.*

INTELLIGENT DESIGN

All levels, floors, and platforms within the station can be reached by lifts or ramps. This design—revolutionary during a time when, according to Sam Roberts, author of *Grand Central: How a Train Station Transformed America*, "lots of people didn't know what a ramp was"—was considered necessary for train passengers with large pieces of luggage.

TRAIN IN VAIN

During World War II, German military intelligence sent two spies to sabotage a basement containing converters used to power all of the trains arriving at and departing from the terminal. The spies were arrested by the FBI before they were able to carry out the task.

YOU'VE DEFINITIVELY ARRIVED

Platform 61 has a concealed entrance and a lift that goes directly to the Waldorf Astoria Hotel. Out of service for some time, this entrance was used to usher magnates arriving in their private rail cars directly into the hotel, as well as President Franklin D. Roosevelt, whose entourage took advantage of the large lift to keep his physical disability under wraps.

I CAN HEAR THE HEART BEATING AS ONE

The terminal transformed midtown Manhattan into a heart capable of powering the world's economic center. Previously, a rail yard that was two blocks wide and ran from 42nd Street to 56th cordoned off the city's center from all commerce and development. By pointing out the development opportunities the station—and the subterranean tracks it could facilitate—would open up, railroad engineer William J. Wilgus got Cornelius Vanderbilt, J. P. Morgan, and other railroad directors to approve his $35 million project and give him carte blanche over the station's construction.

THE PANOPTICON

A look at any one of his films makes it apparent that Stanley Kubrick worked on a different level than other filmmakers. The unorthodox routes he took to extract performances from his actors is one area where this disparity is explicit. In order to get R. Lee Ermey razor-sharp for his impeccable rendition of an unflappable drill sergeant in *Full Metal Jacket*, Kubrick forced Ermey to recite his lines as fast as he could while also catching tennis balls that an assistant director hurled at him. Shelley Duvall's completely unhinged and hysterical performance in *The Shining* was the result of Kubrick intentionally keeping her isolated, refusing to praise her, putting her through an exhausting amount of work (the iconic "baseball bat" scene went through 127 takes, eliciting genuine tears from Duvall), and instructing the crew to ignore her pleas.

THE
BICAMERAL
MIND

According to psychologist Julian Jaynes,
consciousness and the self are relatively new
features of human existence.

MASTER OF YOUR DOMAIN

The basis of Jaynes's theory is that as recently as 3,000 years ago the human mind operated with one part of the brain speaking and the other part obeying.

GOD ONLY KNOWS

Jaynes, who was a professor of psychology at Princeton, suggests that the moments where the voices of the gods break through and guide the characters in *The Iliad* are examples of bicameralism at work. Jaynes also points out that the characters in *The Iliad* completely lack the self-awareness that is a hallmark of consciousness today.

ANCIENT ALIENS

For Jaynes and his adherents, the mystery surrounding the construction of the Pyramids vanishes when recognizing that those who built them were functioning under this bicameral method. When self-awareness and identity are replaced by a hallucinatory mental state where the commanding voice is unquestioningly obeyed, people are capable of exceeding generally accepted human limits. As evidence, Jaynes points to the incredible strength and athleticism that schizophrenics regularly exhibit.

STAND ON THE WORD

The introduction of the written word (Jaynes claims that the Code of Hammurabi was the first publicly displayed writing) is what led to the breakdown of this manner of cognitive function, throwing large portions of the civilized world into complete disarray and dissolution; in support of this anarchic claim, Jaynes cites a 100-year period in Egypt where there is no historical record available despite there being no great invasion and no plague to tie it to. Jaynes also suggests that the Israelites were those who continued to operate under bicameralism and so were cast out of normal society and forced to wander around the desert.

QUINCY JONES

The life of this producer, composer, and musician is nothing short of staggering.

JUST IN TIME

Jones toured with Frank Sinatra and Ray Charles and formed famous partnerships with Miles Davis and Michael Jackson. Eventual victim Jay Sebring invited him to Sharon Tate's house on the night of the Manson Family murders. Jones even played trumpet on Elvis Presley's first #1 record, "Heartbreak Hotel," despite having no affinity for Elvis's abilities ("motherf*cker couldn't sing," Jones told *GQ*). Jones refers to himself as "Ghetto Gump" in light of his eerie knack for being in the thick of the action.

NEVER GOING BACK AGAIN

Jones has never learned how to drive, having been scared off after he was a passenger during an automobile accident at the age of 14. Jones, describing the accident later on, said: "Trailways bus hit us. Everybody in the car died except for me. Reached up and pulled my friend, and his head fell off. . . . It was very traumatic."

COLD-BLOODED

Literary luminary Truman Capote tried to get Jones removed as the score composer for the film adaptation of *In Cold Blood*. Capote "called [director] Richard Brooks . . . and said, 'Richard, I don't understand why you've got a Negro doing the music for a film with no people of color in it,'" according to Jones. But he remained, and the score was nominated for an Academy Award.

LA PETITE MORT

In 1974, Jones had a brain aneurysm that was serious enough for his family and friends to plan a memorial service for him. Jones attended that service with his neurologist. The malady required a clip to be placed on a blood vessel in his brain and forced doctors to tell Jones that he would have to stop playing the trumpet. But he quickly missed playing and kept at it until he blew into the instrument one day and felt a pain in his head. He has not touched a trumpet since, despite missing it so much that he constantly mimes notes on an invisible version of the instrument.

I CAN FEEL YOUR LOOK

The famous double-slit experiment proved that light could display characteristics of both waves and particles. Even stranger, if light is observed it behaves as a particle, and if it is unobserved it behaves as a wave. Strangest of all, it doesn't matter when that observation occurs, as tracking photons once they have already passed through the slits—and should behave as waves—keeps them in particular form, suggesting that the observation can alter events that have already occurred.

MUSEUM
OF BROKEN
RELATIONSHIPS

It seems like something out of postmodern fiction, but this singular exhibition space actually does exist in Zagreb, Croatia.

NO JOKE

When Olinka Vistica and Drazen Grubisic's four-year relationship ended in 2003, they mused that they should start a museum for the items they had amassed during their time together. Three years later, Grubisic contacted Vistica and said that their attempt to ease the pain was actually a brilliant idea and should be pursued in earnest.

WHAT WE TALK ABOUT WHEN WE TALK ABOUT LOVE

The collection of seemingly mundane items is brought to life by captions from the anonymous donors. The tone of these messages ranges from regretful ("I never put them on. The relationship might have lasted longer if I had.") to score-settling ("Darling, should you ever get the ridiculous idea to walk into a cultural institution like a museum for the first time in your life, you'll remember me.").

HOLLYWOOD ENDING

Another location was opened in Los Angeles in June 2016, but it lasted only until November 2017. Try as you might, it's hard not to draw conclusions about the museum's inability to make it in a town that became renowned for its insistence on happy endings.

SWEPT UP IN THE CURRENT

The existence of such an unorthodox museum seems possible only in a world that has been transformed by the individual platforms social media provides. Says Vistica: "We transformed the concept of a museum from that temple about historic things. Museums can be about you and about me. We added some sort of democratic value and introduced love as a tool to learn about the world."

MAGIC
MUSHROOMS

There is seemingly no end to the wonders of fungi.

EVERYTHING IS CONNECTED

Mycologist Paul Stamets has claimed that mycelium is Earth's internet, forming an intricately branched network that provides plants the ability to share nutrients and send out warning signals upon encountering a harmful agent. Not only that, if one branch in the network is broken, the mycelium quickly reroutes the information being transferred through another pathway.

MIND GAMES

It is believed that mushrooms produce the alkaloid psilocybin, which grants over 200 species of mushrooms their psycho-active properties, in order to suppress a neurotransmitter and dampen the appetite of insects, reducing, to some degree, the fungi's chances of being consumed.

THE CURE

Soil that has been polluted by an oil spill can be regenerated if it is injected with mushroom mycelium, with the enzymes turning the hydrocarbons in the oil into carbohydrates that produce mushrooms. Once these mushrooms sporulate, they will attract insects that will bring in birds carrying plant-generating seeds, transforming what should be a wasteland into a flourishing environment in only eight weeks. Strains of the agarikon mushroom have also proven effective against smallpox and flu viruses, so much so that the U.S. Department of Defense has funded research examining the ability of this fungus to combat biological weapons.

GARY RIDGWAY

America's fascination with serial killers got all it could ever ask for with the "Green River Killer," who terrorized the Northwest during the 1980s.

A QUICK ONE WHILE HE'S AWAY

At the age of 16, Ridgway lured a six-year-old boy into the woods and stabbed him in the ribs. The boy survived, much to the surprise of Ridgway, who said: "I always wondered what it would be like to kill," as he walked away laughing.

WHAT IS A NUMBER THAT A MAN SHOULD KNOW IT?

Ridgway confessed to, and was convicted of, killing 49 women, but later boasted that he killed closer to 80. He claimed that he offered up this revision to provide closure to the families of his unidentified victims, but many believe that this is simply the preternaturally deceptive Ridgway's attempt to shore up his infamous legacy.

IT'S NOT A LIE IF YOU BELIEVE IT

Ridgway became a suspect in the case in 1983, and was subjected to a polygraph test in 1984, which he passed. He was not captured until 2001, when DNA linked him to four of the slayings. Melvin Foster, another suspect in the case, actually failed a polygraph test in 1982.

BRIEF INTERVIEWS WITH HIDEOUS MEN

The notorious Ted Bundy was interviewed by Green River Task Force members Robert Keppel and Dave Reichert in connection with the case. Bundy offered opinions on the psychology, motivations, and behavior of the killer, and suggested that they were revisiting the dump sites to have sex with the victims, a hypothesis that turned out to be true.

THIS IS NOT A PHOTOGRAPH

Author and philosopher Susan Sontag—who famously savaged the photographer Diane Arbus's work in the 1973 essay "Freak Show"—and her son were photographed by Arbus in 1965. It is more than tempting to conclude that Sontag's appraisal was colored by a lack of fondness for that particular portrait, as she once wrote: "Through photographs, each family constructs a portrait-chronicle of itself—a portable kit of images that bears witness to its connectedness."

UNKNOWN LEGENDS

In the era of reality television and social media, it seems like anyone can make their way into the public eye, but these unrecognized geniuses are just a sampling of individuals who never received their due.

TERRY CALLIER

His ability to move effortlessly between folk, soul, and jazz probably cost him, as his malleability and unique sound made him difficult to market. But if you want to turn people's heads, toss on the upbeat kiss-off "You Goin' Miss Your Candyman" or the haunting "Spin Spin Spin."

ORIANA FALLACI

She was not perfect, but this Italian journalist was tough (she accused Ariel Sharon of being a terrorist after getting him to define the term), brave (while interviewing Iran's Ayatollah Khomeini she removed the chador women in Iran are forced to wear, calling it a "stupid, medieval rag" to his face), and brilliant (her reflection on Golda Meir and the sacrifices society begs of talented women remains both chilling and relevant). One can't help but wonder what she would be capable of if let loose in the contemporary world during her prime.

ERIC HOFFER

A high school dropout, one-time denizen of Los Angeles's Skid Row, and longtime longshoreman, Hoffer turned a snowy winter with Montaigne's *Essays* into an avalanche of insight. His book *The True Believer* cut to the core of extremist cultural movements and the frustrated souls who participate in them, observing that "a movement is pioneered by men of words," and "materialized by fanatics."

SYLVESTER

You probably recognize the falsetto, since Prince borrowed it on his way to pop immortality. But this brash talent, who ruled San Francisco during the '70s and '80s, never got the acclaim he deserved. Dubious? Take the word of David Bowie, who after a poorly selling 1972 show in San Francisco said that the town did not need him since "They've got Sylvester."

INSTANT
ERUDITION

If you're looking to make maximum impact with an insight, linking it to a profound statement from another is a tried-and-true method. Here are a few that may come in handy.

BUT NOW I SEE

For those momentary flashes where either the truth or the world becomes clear, turn to Anne Carson's *Autobiography of Red*, in which she describes the first meeting of two lovers as "one of those moments that is the opposite of blindness." Carson's writing is full of passages that carry a similar measure of mythic resonance, a fortunate byproduct of her lifelong interest in Greek and Classics.

THE SAGE OF ENNET HOUSE

David Foster Wallace thought more, and better, about the deleterious effects of accessible entertainment than anyone. If someone you know is struggling with screen time, tell them to keep these words in mind when they reach for their phone: "At a certain point, we're gonna have to build some machinery, inside our guts, to help us deal with this. Because the technology is just gonna get better and better and better. And it's gonna get easier and easier, and more and more convenient, and more and more pleasurable, to be alone with images on a screen, given to us by people who do not love us."

If they are susceptible to poetry, you can also try this one from Henry David Thoreau: "As if you could kill time without injuring eternity."

ST. VINCENT

Ever failed to connect with a hyped piece of contemporary art (perhaps Damien Hirst's shark in formaldehyde leaps to mind)? Rene Ricard, writing about Jean-Michel Basquiat for *Artforum*, pointed out that the inclusion of such pieces might be an overcompensation for a previous oversight. "Nobody wants to miss the Van Gogh Boat. The idea of the unrecognized genius slaving away in a garret is a deliciously foolish one. We must credit the life of Vincent Van Gogh for really sending that myth into orbit. How many pictures did he sell. One. He couldn't give them away. Almost no one could bear his work, even among the most modern of his colleagues. . . . We're so ashamed of his life that the rest of art history will be retribution for Van Gogh's neglect. No one wants to be part of a generation that ignores another Van Gogh. . . . There is no great artist in all of art history who was as ignored as Van Gogh, yet people are still afraid of missing the Van Gogh Boat."

JOHN McPHEE

His wide-ranging interests and pitch-perfect prose cause many to speak of him in hushed tones.

QUIZ KID

Celebrated for his inexhaustible curiosity, McPhee has always been exceptionally inquisitive. While an undergraduate at Princeton, McPhee appeared as the "juvenile" panelist once or twice a week on the popular radio and television quiz program *Twenty Questions*.

A SERIOUS MAN

McPhee, who has taught nonfiction writing at Princeton since 1975, does not write during a semester that he teaches, and vice versa. His focus and discipline have paid off, as he won the Pulitzer Prize in 1999 for his book *Annals of the Former World*, and he counts David Remnick (editor-in-chief at the *New Yorker*) and Eric Schlosser (author of *Fast Food Nation* and executive producer of the Academy Award–winning film *There Will Be Blood*) among his flock of disciples.

GARDEN OF
FORKING PATHS

The ornate and original structures that McPhee's pieces have become known for are the result of an involved system. After typing all his notes for a particular piece into his computer, he studies that data and comes up with categories. He assigns each category a code, makes an index card for each one, and rearranges them on a table until the sequence strikes his fancy. Once the data has been labeled with the codes, a computer program called Structur organizes the bits into groups. McPhee then converts each of these groups into his clean, precise prose.

EXPERT WITNESS

McPhee's work routinely concerns itself with immensely passionate experts, such as Henri Vaillancourt in *The Survival of the Bark Canoe* and "Otto," the domineering chef featured in the overlooked but influential "Brigade de Cuisine." McPhee suggests that his attraction to them is due in part to his own introverted nature. (He told the *Washington Post*, "I flunked kindergarten because of shyness.") While McPhee still feels "awkward" and "tongue-tied" despite his considerable stature, the experts' ability to hold court no matter who is around astounds him. "They're so occupied with what they're doing they don't pay any attention."

WICKET PERCEPTIVE

To the uninitiated, the whirl of a cricket match is impossible to understand, much less discuss intelligently. George Orwell made the latter possible with his essay "Raffles and Miss Blandish," using the game to shine a light into the character of his own countrymen. He wrote that cricket "gives expression to a well-marked trait in the English character, the tendency to value 'form' or 'style' more highly than success. In the eyes of any true cricket-lover it is possible for an innings of ten runs to be 'better' (i.e. more elegant) than an innings of a hundred runs: cricket is also one of the very few games in which the amateur can excel the professional. It is a game full of forlorn hopes and sudden dramatic changes of fortune, and its rules are so defined that their interpretation is partly an ethical business."

ROBERT OPPENHEIMER

His wide-ranging brilliance not only allowed the Manhattan Project to succeed—it managed to capture the spiritual significance of the Atomic Age.

CLOUD OF UNKNOWING

While he is best known for the attention to detail and managerial abilities that made the Manhattan Project a success, those skills seemed to evolve later in life. There are reports of a younger Oppenheimer suffering from the aloofness theoretical physicists are famous for; for instance, he did not learn of the 1929 Wall Street crash until six months after the fact.

THE CRUCIBLE

Oppenheimer's insatiable curiosity and openness to a broad spectrum of ideas and the individuals who held them led to his security clearance being revoked during Joseph McCarthy's infamous witch hunt in the 1950s. Researchers later found that although the KGB had attempted to recruit Oppenheimer, he refused to inform on the United States.

I'VE SEEN THINGS YOU PEOPLE WOULDN'T BELIEVE

He published only five papers in his career and never won the Nobel Prize, but Oppenheimer published a paper in 1930 that predicted the existence of the positron. Carl David Anderson would win the Nobel Prize in 1936 after actually discovering the particle.

PICK YOUR POISON

Though undeniably brilliant, as a student Oppenheimer struggled mightily with authority figures. He attempted to poison his tutor while pursuing his doctorate at Cambridge, leaving an apple laced with chemicals from the lab on the tutor's desk. Though he was not punished after his parents lobbied university authorities, Oppenheimer eventually left Cambridge for the University of Göttingen, where he was so domineering in class discussions that a number of students signed a petition threatening to boycott unless he settled down. Professor Max Born presented Oppenheimer with the petition, and he reined himself in.

ON WRITING

There's no arguing that writers are driven by something mysterious. But if you listen closely, they occasionally provide a look behind the curtain.

CIRCLE OF LIFE

A prolific composer, writer, and translator, Paul Bowles seemingly did nothing but create. But his compulsion was powered by a desire for the exact opposite. "Many of my short stories are simple emotional outbursts. They came out all at once, like eggs, and I felt better afterward. In that sense much of my writing is an exhortation to destroy. . . . It is a desire above all to bring about destruction, that's certain," said Bowles in a 1970 interview.

HELP ME
LOSE MY MIND

Don DeLillo has the rare ability to take the reader to a place that feels both impossible and inevitable within a single paragraph. A key to the mysterious logic at work in his writing appears in a 1993 interview with the *Paris Review*, in which DeLillo says: "The words typed on the white page have a sculptural quality. They form odd correspondences. They match up not just through meaning but through sound and look. The rhythm of a sentence will accommodate a certain number of syllables. One syllable too many, I look for another word. . . . I'm completely willing to let language press meaning upon me."

ERNEST IMITATION

While there is little hope of replicating the contradictory combination of detachment and absorption that made her a legend, Joan Didion's style is partially the result of her typing out the novels of Ernest Hemingway as a youth, which she said she did in order "to learn how sentences work."

MYSTERY AND MANNERS

There is no lack of aspiring authors who are so intent on accumulating experiences to mine that they never get around to actually sitting down and writing. If only they had listened to Flannery O'Connor, who spent a majority of her life on a farm in rural Georgia: "The fact is that anybody who has survived his childhood has enough information about life to last him the rest of his days."

IT TAKES A LOT TO LAUGH, IT TAKES A TRAIN TO CRY

"Mussolini made the trains run on time," has become a sardonic reminder to look at the positives of having to deal with overbearing individuals. The phrase was also uttered ironically upon its coinage, as Italian dictator Benito Mussolini's emphasis on order was far too focused on causing misery to get railway service up to speed. Though Mussolini took credit for improved train transportation during his reign, Italian railway service remained unreliable despite considerable improvements—which were already in place before Mussolini seized power.

ELLIOTT SMITH

Everything but songwriting was a struggle for Smith, who took his own life in 2003.

THIS IS HOW WE WALK ON THE MOON

The famously reticent musician agreed to play the nominated "Miss Misery" at the 1998 Academy Awards only after producers informed him that the song would be performed by Richard Marx if Smith refused to appear. He later said of the experience, "I wouldn't want to live in that world, but it was fun to walk around on the moon for a day."

TAKE A SAD SONG

He was supposed to contribute a cover of the Beatles' "Hey Jude" for the Wes Anderson film *The Royal Tenenbaums.* But Smith's depression had reached the point where he was unable to submit the track in time, leaving everyone who heard his glorious cover of "Because" in *American Beauty* to speculate on the majesty of what could have been.

I'M NOT DOWN

Smith didn't see his wrenching, heartfelt songs as dark or sad, and once said, "I'd be really happy if I could write a song as universal and accessible as 'I Second That Emotion.' It's a big game to play, trying to make something that's mainstream enough and still *human*." However, it is telling, and tragic, that he chose a song with that particular title—even when Smith was gesturing toward pop music the weight of his interior life couldn't help but make itself known.

ACCIDENTAL DISCOVERIES

Never underestimate humanity's knack for stumbling into something huge while trying to get somewhere else.

I'M SO TIRED

Charles Goodyear had been trying to make rubber more durable for years, but he only succeeded when he accidentally dropped his rubber concoction on a hot stove while performing an experiment. The result was a charred, leathery material with a flexible edge that made rubber weatherproof. Tragically, Goodyear never benefited from his discovery and died $200,000 in debt.

GIVE A PLASTIC FORM TO FORMLESS THINGS

Leo Baekeland was searching for a replacement for shellac—an expensive resin secreted by a particular species of beetle—when he combined formaldehyde, phenol, and other materials. This produced a heat-resistant polymer that Baekeland christened "Bakelite," but which is more commonly known as plastic.

THE SOUND OF
THE COSMOS

In 1964, while working with the Holmdel antenna in New Jersey, two astronomers named Robert Wilson and Arno Penzias heard a puzzling noise. After ruling out possible interference from urban areas, nuclear tests, or pigeons nesting in the antenna, Wilson and Penzias came across Robert Dicke's theory that radiation left over from a universe-generating big bang would now act as background cosmic radiation. They realized that this was the noise they were hearing and went on to receive a Nobel Prize.

HUMAN,
ALL TOO HUMAN

While searching for an elixir that would provide eternal life, Chinese alchemists ended up in an ironic realm that is typically the stuff of Greek tragedies: they found that mixing salt peter, sulfur, and charcoal is a recipe for gunpowder, not immortality.

THE BOXER REBELLION

The catchy name has it on the tip of many tongues, but few know the details of this convoluted international affair.

SEEDS OF DISCORD

The rebellion was launched by a group of Chinese known as the Righteous Fists of Harmony, who rose up against the Western influences that the Qing dynasty had allowed to enter China. A period of severe drought caused tensions to explode, as many Chinese blamed the Westerners for cursing their land. The Chinese were also furious over missionary activity in the country, and European legations not being subject to Chinese authorities, a loophole that they readily took advantage of.

THIS SH*T'S CHESS, IT AIN'T CHECKERS

With the rebellion underway, the empress dowager Cixi publicly declared war on the foreign powers but also told General Ronglu, leader of the Imperial Army, to protect the foreign legations that were being besieged. Ronglu mainly followed this directive, but he also had his men fire on the legations to satisfy the conservatives in the court. Ronglu also worked against the Boxers, attacking them, denying their commander, Dong Fuxiang, artillery that would have enabled him to destroy the foreign legations, and hiding an imperial decree that ordered Imperial General Nie Shicheng to stop fighting the rebels.

SILVER LINING

The Chinese were required to pay reparations for the losses stemming from the rebellion, and the United States used a large portion of the money it received for the Boxer Indemnity Scholarship Fund, which paid for the education of Chinese students in U.S. universities. The recipients of these scholarships include Yang Chen-Ning, winner of the Nobel Prize in Physics; architectural engineer Edward Y. Ying, who was influential in the planning of modern Shanghai; and the innovative writer Chen Hengzhe.

PRECEDENT OF THE UNITED STATES

American historian Walter LaFeber has pointed out that President William McKinley's decision to send troops to China without consulting Congress or declaring war was the creation of a new executive power, one that McKinley's successor, Teddy Roosevelt, readily employed and rendered commonplace for future presidents.

MEMORY

The mystery of the human brain is largely wrapped up in this activity that is equal parts blessing and curse.

HERACLITUS KNEW

A memory is the result of nerve cells firing or responding to one another at an elevated rate without further increased stimulation. This causes the brain to pay attention and build a synaptic connection, meaning that with each new experience or signal, the brain rewires itself, either strengthening an existing link or building another.

SET ADRIFT ON MEMORY BLISS

Scientists believe that the hippocampus, of which humans have two, is largely responsible for memory by determining the value of sensory phenomena. This belief results from the strange case of Henry Gustav Molaison, who had his hippocampi removed in 1953 and could no longer make memories despite still being able to perform well on IQ tests.

EVERYTHING IN ITS RIGHT PLACE

The idea of constructing a mind palace, taking advantage of the strength of spatial memory by placing objects or information in a real or imagined place, was ushered into the public consciousness by Sherlock Holmes. But this mnemonic device actually dates back to ancient Greece and Rome, and is mentioned in Cicero's *De Oratore*. Also, the common phrase "in the first place" is believed to be a vestige of the widespread employment of this technique.

THE PAST
ISN'T EVEN PAST

The idea that memories, primarily traumatic ones, can be transmitted through generations has gained steam in recent years, as studies show that an ancestor's experiences can affect the genetic code and mental functioning of their descendants. These are known as epigenetic changes, which do not rewrite DNA but rather affect how it is read, emphasizing different aspects embedded within the coding.

MAKE AMERICA
EUROPEAN AGAIN

For a number of reasons, 1951 to 1963 in America seems like a period that conservatives would want to try and return to—until you realize that the top income tax rate was 91 percent. President Kennedy advocated for a cut before his death, arguing that tax rates were too high and tax revenues too low, but the top rate remained above 70 percent until 1981, when Ronald Reagan cut it to 50 percent. Reagan then cut it to 28 percent in 1986, a low that makes the current top rate of 37 percent feel nothing short of Soviet to some Americans.

FIONA
APPLE

*As brilliant as she is unpredictable, she never
fails to reward one's interest.*

WON'T BACK DOWN

From listening to her music, it is clear that Apple possesses a powerful sensitivity, particularly for someone in the public eye. And it is not as though she tunes out the inevitable criticism in order to get by: the full title of her second album, popularly known as *When the Pawn...*, is a 90-word poem Apple composed after reading letters in *Spin* that cast her in a negative light.

CRIMINALLY FAST BRILLIANCE

Apple wrote "Criminal," the biggest hit off her debut album, *Tidal*, in 45 minutes after Sony asked for a reliable single that could provide the new artist a breakout song.

NOT A PARENT

Apple has been known to carry the book *Raising Happiness, 10 Simple Steps for More Joyful Kids and Happier Parents* with her. She does not have kids, and says, "I've never wanted kids. But I do read about parenting a lot. For some reason it's very interesting to me—I think because I'm just big on self-parenting."

PYRRHIC VICTORY

Apple's early career was marred by a famous rant at the MTV Awards, which included her saying "this world is bullsh*t." Asked about that moment later on, Apple displayed the honesty and insight that make her such a compelling force: "I felt that I deserved recognition but that the recognition I was getting was for the wrong reasons. I felt that now, in the blink of an eye, all of those people who didn't give a f*ck who I was, or what I thought, were now all at once just humoring, appeasing me, and not because of my talent, but instead because of the fact that somehow, with the help of my record company, and my makeup artist, my stylist and my press, I had successfully created the illusion that I was perfect and pretty and rich, and therefore living a higher quality of life. . . . I'd saved myself from misfit status, but I'd betrayed my own kind by becoming a paper doll in order to be accepted."

JOAN OF ARC

Her miraculous life and tragic death both seemed under the influence of something beyond this realm.

BOY, THAT ESCALATED QUICKLY

Armagnac forces had been under siege at Orleans for five months when Joan arrived on the scene. In the following days they routed the British in a series of offensives and began to claw their way out of the tremendous hole that had caused them to place their fate in the hands of an illiterate peasant girl.

MORE HUMAN THAN HUMAN

Despite spending her life in rural France, Joan took to things with incredible alacrity, and her abilities in horse riding and military strategy were quickly advanced enough for her to sit, and be accepted, at the head of the French Army. Her prowess as a strategist was so impressive that her maneuvers are studied to this day at École spéciale militaire de Saint-Cyr, the leading French military academy. She also showed incredible bravery and invulnerability, returning to one battle after getting wounded in the neck by an arrow, and surviving a large stone falling on her head in another.

DRACONIAN DRESS CODE

Her claims of receiving divine visions brought her to the attention of the Catholic Church, but the heretical act she was convicted of and executed for was cross-dressing. Joan had initially assumed male dress in order to sneak through territory held by the British on her way to Orleans, and she had assumed the garb again as a prisoner in order to protect herself against rape.

THE PUBLIC FORGIVES EVERYTHING EXCEPT GENIUS

The wisdom Joan exhibited during her trial has wowed scholars and artists for centuries. A particularly impressive moment comes when the inquisitors ask if she knew herself to be in God's grace. "Yes" would bring a charge of heresy; "no" would be admitting that she did not have the visions she claimed, relegating her to a state of sin. Instead, she responded with "If I am not, may God put me there; and if I am, may God so keep me," exhibiting the swift subtlety that is the mark of true genius, and eliciting gasps from those who believed they had her cornered.

GMOs

There is considerable evidence that genetically modified organisms do not negatively impact individual health. What those who eagerly cite such studies fail to realize is that an absence of evidence is not proof that GMOs are harmless and risk-free. There is no way to test what could occur when these entities are introduced into a complex framework such as the ecosystem, where one unforeseen interaction could have catastrophic results.

REMAIN
IN LIGHT

By focusing on what allows us to see instead of what we are seeing, the work of these artists proves to be immensely illuminating.

BOUND FOR GLORY

James Turrell's motivation to construct a temple of perception (see page 168) is born out of his lifelong devotion to light, space, and the very act of perceiving. Believing that "light is not so much something that reveals, as it is itself the revelation," Turrell has created works that make light seem tangible and solid, provide well-worn colors with shocking vibrancy, and can make one feel as though they are hallucinating, being provided with a glimpse of the afterlife, or getting a look at the universe as it was before there was any means of conceiving what it was.

NOBODY WOULD PAINT LIKE THAT IF THEY COULD SEE

Light artists such as Turrell, Robert Irwin, and Dan Flavin owe a huge debt to the Impressionists, in particular Claude Monet, who was so heavily focused on capturing the constant variance he perceived in sunlight that critics claimed he "invented light." His obsession not only changed the way the world sees—it cemented subjectivity as the primary concern of artistic expression.

AT PLAY IN THE FIELDS OF THE LORD

Lighting is such a large concern for filmmakers that Martin Scorsese said, "Light is at the core of who we are." And no director has mastered it to the degree Terrence Malick has. Whether it be the stark glare of *Badlands*, the unequaled splendor of *Days of Heaven*, or the meditative pall present in *The Tree of Life*, the deeply philosophical Malick (he translated Martin Heidegger's *The Essence of Reasons* from German to English as a graduate student) is a master at capturing the glory that frames existence and its attendant horrors.

RANKED-CHOICE VOTING

Some see this as the only antidote to the problems American democracy is currently facing.

A VOTE FOR
AND AGAINST

In an overwhelming majority of state and national elections, the current system of voting frequently allows candidates to win with less than an outright majority of votes, which can lead to elected officials whom a majority of voters oppose. Ranked-choice voting, in which voters rank each of the candidates according to their preference, prevents such outcomes.

JUST GIVE ME A SECOND

The system works as follows: the first choices listed on the collected ballots are counted, and if a candidate receives an outright majority, they win. If there is no majority, the candidate with the fewest first choices is eliminated and voters who ranked that candidate first receive credit for their second choice. The process continues and last-place candidates are eliminated until one candidate reaches a majority. A second choice counts only if the first choice has been eliminated.

BEST OF ALL POSSIBLE WORLDS

The practice provides a salve for a number of issues that currently exist in the political world. By removing candidates who cannot win, voters can cast their ballot for whomever they want, rather than settle for the lesser of two evils in an attempt to keep a candidate they find particularly odious out of office. Since a second ranking is worth seeking out and last-place rankings are to be avoided, it is also believed that candidates would court a wider spectrum of voters and be far less likely to participate in negative campaigning, as it may alienate an opponent's supporters.

NEW ORDER

While it is just beginning to garner widespread attention in the United States, ranked-choice voting has actually been around since the 19th century. It is related to the concept of Single Transferable Vote that an English lawyer named Thomas Hare advocated for in the 1860s. The practice was rapidly adopted in Australia and Ireland, where it is used to this day in national elections. The measure was also nearly adopted by the South Carolina legislature following the Civil War, when it appeared that whites would lose the control they'd grown accustomed to. They decided against it and soon went in a very different direction, erecting the discriminatory edifice that would come to be known as Jim Crow.

A LEAGUE OF THEIR OWN

Even if you're not a fan, there are a few athletes whose exploits transcend the sports page.

WHEN THE MAN COMES AROUND

For six glorious years, every start Pedro Martinez made for the Boston Red Sox was a mixture of religious revival and rock concert. In his prime, the diminutive Martinez was better than anyone ever was, using an incomparable combination of pitches, command, and power to dominate an era when PED-fueled offenses held sway (his 1.74 ERA during the 2000 campaign came at a time when the league average was 4.92). A pitcher so incandescent that the legendary writer David Halberstam said he was "something rarer still—a genuine artist," Martinez showed the Boston franchise and its beleaguered fan base a way out of the cursed, barren expanse where they dwelt for nearly a century.

TOWER OF MEANING

The beguiling combination of uncontrollable rage and Buddha-level acceptance for both the rhythm a particular game took, and the sacrifices required by a team. The breathtaking and completely unblockable turnaround jumper. The peerless post defense. The unsurpassed comedic instincts, which helped usher "ball don't lie" into the lexicon. Rasheed Wallace never averaged 20 points or 10 rebounds a game for an entire season, and he never made an All-NBA team, and yet an alarming number of his peers will cite him when discussing the most talented guy they ever played against. 'Sheed never dominated in the manner one would have expected considering his massive ability, but few individuals have held such sway in the hearts and minds of other players and fans.

MEMENTO MORI

While he has played the game at a level that brought David Foster Wallace and many other fans to their knees, perhaps the most impressive aspect of Roger Federer's tennis career is his capacity to do what almost no great athlete can—accept that they are mortal. Federer's willingness to recognize his slightly reduced abilities as he moved into his mid-30s and make the necessary adjustments has allowed him to remain on top of the men's game, despite rarely reaching the transcendent heights he once did. After years when it seemed he was concerned more with a Platonic form of the game than his opponent, Federer's recent play reflects an understanding that he does not have to be perfect to win, he simply has to be better than the individual across from him—a startling bit of humility from someone accustomed to immaculate performance.

THAT'S GOLD, JERRY

The Golden Ratio (1.618 . . . or phi, which is a representation of two quantities if their ratio is the same as the ratio of their sum to the larger of the two quantities) is a wonder that pops up throughout the universe: the arrangement of petals in a red rose, the paintings of Dalí and Mondrian, the structure of galaxies, and the spiralled shells of mollusks. But the uncovering of this miracle was not welcomed by all. The Pythagoreans, who were powered by the belief that the world is neat and orderly, were furious upon hearing that the famous Golden Ratio was an irrational number (it contains no common measure and so cannot be written as a whole number or simple fraction), with the individual who broke the news "so hated that not only was he banned from [the Pythagoreans'] common association and way of life, but even his tomb was built, as if [their] former colleague was departed from life among humankind," according to the Greek philosopher and historian Iamblichus.

BEDS MADE
BY THE CIA

As evidenced by these international imbroglios, gathering intelligence is a world away from exercising it.

SYRIA

There is some debate about the exact nature of U.S. involvement in Husni al-Za'im overthrowing the democratically elected government of Shukri al-Quwatli in 1949. But the construction of the Trans-Arabian Pipeline—the main American objective in Syria—was approved by al-Za'im just over a month after the coup, despite the matter having previously gained little traction in Syrian parliament.

IRAN

Mohammad Mosaddeq, who, as prime minister, nationalized the Iranian oil industry (wresting control away from what is now BP) and installed a number of social programs to help the poor, was overthrown by the CIA at the request of British intelligence in 1953. The coup transferred power to an authoritarian ruler who needed U.S. support to enact the policies that engendered the Islamic Revolution of 1979.

IRAQ

In 1959, Iraqi prime minister Abd al-Karim Qasim survived an assassination attempt that is reported to have been a collaboration between the CIA and Egyptian intelligence. A young Saddam Hussein was cited as the reason the attempt failed, as he was only supposed to provide cover but instead fired on Qasim. Despite spoiling the endeavor, Hussein's role provided him with widespread exposure and became a crucial part of his image during his rise to power.

AFGHANISTAN

From 1979 to 1989, the U.S. government secretly provided $800 million in weapons and funding for the mujahideen, factions of jihadi guerillas in Afghanistan who were fighting the Afghan government and the Soviet military forces that supported it. The group that later became the Taliban was among the jihadis supported by the U.S. As if that wasn't damning enough, there are also claims that some CIA-funded militants later became part of Al Qaeda, including Osama bin Laden.

RELATIVITY

Perspective is everything when contemplating the laws of the universe.

DOES IT GET EASIER?

The central idea of general relativity, that gravity causes spacetime to curve in a manner that affects the motion of matter, has been beautifully boiled down by American physicist John Archibald Wheeler: "Spacetime tells matter how to move; matter tells spacetime how to curve."

JUST ABOVE OUR HEADS

While some aspects of relativity are only relevant at extremes that occur far outside the plane of human existence, it does not take much to affect time flow rates, which are slower in stronger gravitational fields. Atomic clocks have shown conclusively that the weaker gravitational field 10 kilometers above the Earth's surface (less than the typical cruising altitude of a commercial airplane) causes time to flow faster than at sea level.

TIMES ARE A-CHANGING

Speed is the other variable that affects the flow of time, with the lapse between two events depending on the relative speeds of the observers' frames of reference. This phenomenon is also known as the "twin paradox": a twin who departs Earth in a spaceship traveling near the speed of light and returns 25 years later will find that their twin sibling has aged much more.

UNQUANTIFIABLE

While Einstein's theory of general relativity has been confirmed, it still cannot be reconciled with quantum mechanics because a messenger particle (i.e. the photons in an electromagnetic field) has not been found for gravity. Researchers do believe that one exists, but this "graviton," upon which string theory and many unified theories depend, continues to evade detection.

THE CAUSES OF WORLD WAR I

Often overshadowed by the conflict it created, the Great War connects different eras and peoples like few other events.

MOMENTS SNAP TOGETHER LIKE MAGNETS

History classes always mention the assassination of Austrian archduke Franz Ferdinand by Serbian nationalists and then move on, but in actuality it was Serbia's refusal to investigate the incident that escalated matters. This refusal led to a breakdown of diplomatic relations and caused Russia and Serbia to mobilize their militaries. Austria-Hungary declared war, a move that triggered the preexisting alliances between Germany and Austria-Hungary, France and Russia, and Britain, France, and Belgium.

THE DEADLIEST OF ALL

A half century of relative peace prior to the war allowed Europeans to hold on to the delusion that their particular country was supreme in cultural, economic, and military matters. Seeing the war as an opportunity to prove what they felt to be true, many countries eagerly joined the fray, entirely unaware of the horrors the Industrial Revolution had ushered in to modern warfare.

IT'S RIGHT THERE
IN THE NAME

Powerful German chancellor Otto von Bismarck acquired his authority by conducting successful wars against Denmark, Austria, and France in the 19th century. After that, nothing he did could be challenged. Parliament was neutered, and Bismarck threatened to step down whenever his moves were questioned. Once he was dispatched by Kaiser Wilhelm II in 1890, there was no political infrastructure to stop the combative "New Course" that the Kaiser placed Germany upon. As Michael White said in *The Guardian*, "Bismarck had built a racing car only he could drive."

TOMORROW NEVER KNOWS

Germany's overwhelming embrace of nationalism and militarism was a product of their tremendous need to make up for the humiliations they suffered at the hands of Napoleon during his romp through Western Europe. Treating them as little more than serfs, Napoleon redrew the map of still divided German states and incorporated 36 of them into the Confederation of the Rhine, forcing them to maintain substantial armies for their own defense and supply France with a considerable amount of military personnel.

PRIVILEGED POSITION

The Beatles' sudden development from rulers of the bubble gum set to revolutionary experimentalists is typically chalked up to their genius and their experiments with psychedelics and Eastern thought. But the always-astute Nina Simone, in a 1968 interview with *DownBeat* magazine, pointed out that the band's early success afforded them an exceedingly rare opportunity in the music world, saying: "They have just discovered that they have talent, friend. Fate was good enough to give them time to think about their talent, to develop it as they please, without fighting everybody around them."

MARSHALL McLUHAN

An uncanny ability to identify the currents present in contemporary society took this staid academic far beyond the ivory tower.

PROTECT YA NECK

His unparalleled capacity to anticipate the effects of mass media and recognize patterns in the seemingly chaotic swirl of everyday society may have been fueled by an anatomical anomaly: McLuhan had two arteries pumping blood into his brain, a trait that is primarily found in felines and is exceedingly rare in human beings. The abnormal structure was discovered when an angiogram revealed that his carotid artery was blocked, an issue that would have been catastrophic if not for his extraordinary internal architecture.

THE WORLD GROWS COLD, THE HEATHEN RAGE

McLuhan's concept of the "Global Village" is often seen as anticipating the internet, and his thoughts on what awaited us there ended up being frighteningly prescient. In *The Gutenberg Galaxy*, McLuhan writes: "Instead of tending towards a vast Alexandrian library, the world becomes a computer, and as our senses have gone outside us, Big Brother goes inside. So, unless aware of this dynamic, we shall at once move into a phase of panic terrors, exactly befitting a small world of tribal drums, total interdependence, and superimposed co-existence. The next medium will include television as its content, not as its environment, and will transform television into an art form." In an interview, McLuhan also predicted the combative tone that marks a high number of exchanges on the web, saying, "When people get close together, they get more and more savage, impatient with each other. The global village is a place of very arduous interfaces and very abrasive situations."

CONTEXT IS KING

McLuhan's famous utterance "the medium is the message" is much better known than understood. In essence, it details the technological society's inclination to make context more valuable than content, and for methods of communication to increasingly define the cultural conversation. Using an instance detailed on page 178 as an example, *Time* (a nationwide publication) writing about the Hells Angels (a small motorcycle gang situated in California) stirring up mischief in a small town makes the group seem like a much bigger deal—and greater threat—than the actual elements detailed in the story suggest.

SURFING

This pursuit is widely admired but little understood outside of the cabal of practitioners.

WAVE OF MUTILATION

The record for the world's largest wave surfed is held by Brazilian Rodrigo Koxa, who mustered the nerve to take on and flawlessly navigate an 80-foot-tall wave in Portugal on November 8, 2017. For perspective: a 10-foot-tall wave that is 20 feet long weighs about 410 tons, which is equal to approximately 315 small cars.

CLOSER TO GOD

Thanks to movies like *Point Break*, the spiritual side of surfing has become something of a punch line. But it is a fundamental piece of the pursuit, with early devotees in Hawaii uttering prayers and making offerings before using the wood of the sacred koa tree to construct their boards.

BIRTH OF THE COOL

Surfing's association with the unassailably cool is due in large part to George Freeth, who helped popularize the sport in the U.S. after providing surfing demonstrations in Southern California. Freeth was featured in Jack London's *The Cruise of the Snark*, in which the famous author called Freeth "a sea-god . . . a brown Mercury . . . a member of the kingly species that has mastered matter."

BARBARIAN AT THE GATE

The poet laureate of surfing is journalist William Finnegan, whose pieces for the *New Yorker* and his memoir *Barbarian Days* have provided the sport with enough intellectual ballast to withstand any skepticism. A large part of the reason Finnegan's work stands out is his unflinching, introspective eye. Instead of celebrating his exploits and trumpeting his glorious lifestyle—as most in his position do— Finnegan laments who he was while trotting the globe in search of the ideal wave, saying: "In an inescapable way, we sucked, and we knew it."

I WANT TO PREACH THE WORD, I WANT TO PREACH TO BIRDS

The boundless passion of bird watchers has given rise to a number of poetic collective nouns for groups of a particular bird. You may never wake at dawn to go birding, but knowing that a group of killdeer is a season, a bunch of nightingales a watch, a collection of owls a parliament, a group of crows a murder, a mass of mockingbirds an echo, a gang of parrots a pandemonium, and a flock of flamingoes a flamboyance will make it seem like you're far from a stranger to the avian world.

COLOR

*It is so fundamental to our view of the world
that we fail to see what it actually is.*

I'LL BE YOUR MIRROR

Isaac Newton was the first to determine that color is not inherent in objects, and instead originates in light. The surface of an object reflects some colors and absorbs all the others, and humans perceive only the reflected ones. An object appears white when it reflects all wavelengths and black when it absorbs them all.

LOSING MY EDGE

Your peripheral vision is less colorful and less clear than your vision straight on because rods, which are more sensitive to dim light and transmit mostly black-and-white phenomena to the brain, are most highly concentrated around the edge of the retina.

WHERE'S THAT RED ONE GONNA GO?

The evolution of the ability to see red developed in humans and other primates largely as a result of switching to daytime as the primary period of activity. Beginning to consume fruits, and a need to judge their ripeness, is believed to be another factor.

THE MATRIX

There is considerable variation among cultures as to how many colors are recognized, but the patterns in the evolution of what is described are startlingly consistent. The *World Color Survey*, which looked at color-related terms in languages all across the globe, determined that all cultures have a word for "black" and another for "white." If there is a third color-related term, it is for "red." "Yellow" or "green" is the fourth term, should there be one, with the other receiving the fifth descriptor if the language chooses to acknowledge one. Should the language go beyond this, "blue" is the next color to be singled out.

JOSEPHINE BAKER

On stage, on the frontlines, even on the home front, she was always larger than life.

WATCH THE THRONE

Baker was not bashful about leading the lavish life her talents afforded her. At one point, she had a gold piano and Marie Antoinette's actual bed in her home, as well as a pet cheetah that sported a diamond-encrusted collar.

THE PAYBACK

At the onset of World War II, Baker worked tirelessly to help support France. After performing, Baker would make beds at a homeless shelter and bathe the elderly. She also spied for the French Resistance, conveying messages in invisible ink on the sheet music she carried while touring and smuggling secret photos of German military installations in her underwear, confident that her considerable fame would keep anyone from requesting a strip search. She rose to the rank of lieutenant in the Free French Air Force and was the first American woman to receive the Croix de Guerre.

GOOD INTENTIONS PAVING CO.

The biggest show Baker ever put on was adopting 12 children from all over the world and maintaining the language, dress, customs, and religion of their native countries while raising them at Les Milandes, her castle in southwestern France. Born out of her desire to "prove that human beings can respect each other if given the chance," Baker opened up her home to the public and carefully orchestrated the family dynamics that were on display, a production that made the children feel like "pet monkeys," according to one member of the group. To no one's surprise, the youths began to resist Baker's constant coordination as they matured. With frustrations mounting and resources running low, Baker slowly dismantled her utopian project, sending some of the children to live with her ex-husband Jo Bouillon, others to boarding schools, and a small group to stay with one of her longtime fans in the UK.

WAY OF THE PILGRIM

If someone's feeling stuck creatively and looking for a bit of inspiration, alert them to any of these contemporary meccas.

EVERYBODY KNOWS THIS IS NOWHERE

The landscape will be recognizable to fans of *There Will Be Blood* and *No Country for Old Men*, but they may be surprised that such desolation is near Marfa, Texas, a chic hub of contemporary art. Artist Donald Judd began the transformation when he moved to the town in 1977 in an effort to get away from the inauthenticity of the New York art world. In 1979, he purchased a nearby 340-acre tract of land that included the abandoned buildings of the former U.S. military base Fort D. A. Russell. This property now contains classic minimalist works created by Judd and Robert Irwin, as well as installations from light artist Dan Flavin that critic Michael Kimmelman of the *New York Times* called "the last great work of 20th-century American art."

THE IDEA IS EVERYTHING

No matter what else is on display on the sprawling campus that contains the Massachusetts Museum of Contemporary Art, the star of the show is housed in Building #7: a retrospective of wall drawings from conceptual giant Sol LeWitt. The glorious results of LeWitt's motivating theory—that the artist's idea, not the execution, is all that matters—adorn the 27,000-square-foot warehouse, put there by assistants who were trained to follow the simple instructions left behind by the master.

A GOD-SHAPED HOLE

Just north of Flagstaff, Arizona, the artist James Turrell (see page 122) has been working since 1974 to transform a volcanic crater into an enormous naked-eye observatory that captures his lifelong obsession with light and space. Cynics frequently chuckle at the mythic version of Turrell that circulates—which includes him flying a plane around the Western U.S., landing in the wilderness, and sleeping under the wing— but there is no one who can say that his massive Roden Crater project doesn't inspire such fancies.

DREAMER OF THE GOLDEN DREAM

The Watts Towers is a collection of 17 interconnected towers, architectural structures, individual sculptures, and mosaics designed and built by Sabato "Simon" Rodia. Rodia started on the project when he was 42, despite having no art training and little skill beyond the basic tasks that he picked up while working as a general laborer. Working without a predetermined design and a desire only to build "something big," Rodia improvised the entire way, utilizing hand tools, steel rebar, concrete, and found objects. A number of individuals have been influenced by the work, most famously the legendary composer and bandleader Charles Mingus, who encountered the Towers as a neighborhood youth and claimed it heavily influenced his willingness to improvise, tear down what was, and improve upon it.

VIRGINIA
WOOLF

*As both writer and feminist, few individuals
cast a larger shadow.*

NO LINE BETWEEN LIFE AND LITERATURE

The dazzling turns of mind and commitment to follow them aren't just a feature of her writing. Woolf's husband, Leonard, originally proposed in 1909 but received no answer. He asked again in January 1912 and was rejected outright. Leonard continued his pursuit, to which Virginia responded by saying, "I will not think of my marriage as a profession. The only people who know of it, all think it suitable; and that makes me scrutinize my own motives all the more. . . . I'm half afraid of myself. I sometimes feel that no one ever has or ever can share something." Less than a month later, Virginia said that she wished to marry him.

REVOLUTIONARY ROAD

The impact of her work was not immediate; this is from the *New York Times* review of her debut, *The Voyage Out*: "aside from a certain cleverness . . . there is little in this offering to make it stand out from the ruck of mediocre novels." But within just five years she'd found her stride, with the *Times* likening her writing in *Mrs Dalloway* to "the development of a symphony. It is incredible that this could be done with English prose."

THIS IS THE SHOW, AND WE'RE NOT GONNA CHANGE IT

While Leonard credited his wife's inheritance as the key to her startling development, and Virginia—who struggled with depression throughout her life—cited the peace writing provided as the source of her zealous practice, the occasion of her starting her own press should not be overlooked as a reason for her undeniable originality. By establishing Hogarth Press, through which she also published early works by Katherine Mansfield and T. S. Eliot, Virginia was assured that her writing would see the light of day, a luxury that allowed her to focus on nothing more than articulating the exceptional thoughts and processes occurring in her mind.

HE IS THE
VOICE I HEAR

Between the snarl and swagger, the location ("Gatlinburg in mid-July"), and a man's ultra-hard exterior giving way to considerable sentiment, "A Boy Named Sue," feels like the definitive Johnny Cash song. Only he didn't write it. It is the work of popular cartoonist Shel Silverstein, who is best known as the author of *Where the Sidewalk Ends.* Silverstein wrote the song after a conversation with radio personality Jean Shepherd, whose stories inspired the ubiquitous and divisive holiday classic *A Christmas Story.*

HELLS
ANGELS

This small band of ne'er-do-wells has long loomed large in the American consciousness.

DEVIL'S IN THE DETAILS

Most people, and the OED, toss an apostrophe between the second *l* and the *s* in *Hells*. But there isn't one, yet another rule the rebellious outfit thumbs its nose at. The odd appellation has drawn enough attention that the group addresses it on its website, and Angels have been known to confront and correct reporters who use the apostrophe in an article.

JUDECCA

As a counter to the U.S. Department of Justice's categorization that the club is an organized crime syndicate, the Angels maintain that any crimes committed by members are the responsibility of those individuals and have nothing to do with the club as a whole. But it can't be said that those acts are entirely disavowed. Certain members have been seen with a "Filthy Few" patch on their club leathers, which are believed to be awarded to those who have committed or are prepared to commit murder on behalf of the club.

FAKE NEWS

Hunter S. Thompson, whose career was launched with the help of his profile of, and beating at the hands of, the Hells Angels, saw the group as a phenomenon largely created by the media. In March 1965, the *New York Times*, *Time*, and *Newsweek* all ran articles featuring an overblown synopsis of an incident in Porterville, California, and framed the Angels as a gang of marauders ready to sweep the nation. At that time, "the club's own head count listed roughly eighty-five, all in California. . . . The Hell's [sic] Angels as they exist today were virtually created by *Time*, *Newsweek* and *The New York Times*," Thompson wrote.

STEVIE WONDER

Everybody knows him, but with his inimitable ability to make music that is both joyful and conceptually sophisticated, Stevie can never be talked about too much.

HE SEES THE LIGHT

His blindness was caused by an overabundance of oxygen in his incubator after being born six weeks premature. While many would see this as a bad break, Wonder believes that it is a gift from God, saying it enables him to "go through things that are relatively insignificant, and you pick out things that are more important."

HIGHER GROUND

Ira Tucker, who worked as Wonder's assistant at one time, articulated the difference between Wonder and mere mortals: "When I get stoned and listen to the radio and then I can pick up things. He's there all the time." Interestingly, Wonder claims to have been completely sober after trying marijuana once as a young man and feeling "like I'd lost part of my brain."

FUNKY DRUMMER

Those innovative fills and slinky cymbals that stand out on his albums? That's all Wonder, whose work as a drummer is a tremendously underrated part of his musical ability. Eric Clapton has said "Stevie Wonder has to be the greatest drummer of our time," and Bob Margouleff, who co-produced *Innervisions*, says Wonder's proficiency on the drums is equivalent to that of his songwriting and piano playing.

WHERE IS MY MIND?

While the incredible potential contained in the human mind is well known, these oddities suggest that we have just scratched the surface of its capabilities.

MY LITTLE MAN'S AN IDIOT

Even following your gut isn't what it used to be, as a number of biases have wormed their way into our decision-making process. So the next time you're making a big decision, don't let yourself get held back by an inclination known as anchoring, which is granting recently acquired information outsize importance. Also, keep this in mind the next time you see someone you like pushing into something that seems beyond them, such as politics: they are attempting to capitalize on the halo effect, which is the tendency to assume someone will thrive in other arenas if we already view them positively in one.

THERE'S A NAME FOR THAT

An awareness of Baader-Meinhof phenomenon is particularly important for the readers of a book like this, as it describes the slightly paranoiac sensation of something you just became aware of suddenly popping up everywhere. Of course, it is only because you are finally aware enough to notice it, and after a few instances you start to convince yourself that something spooky is at work.

YOU HAVE NO FAITH IN MEDICINE

The placebo effect, which is an individual's medical condition improving based on their belief that a drug has been administered, is well known. But there is also a downside to the effect: when a placebo is administered to a recipient who has an expectation of it having a negative impact, they will tend to report a negative effect and/or worsening of symptoms. Also, warning patients about the side effects of a particular drug can contribute to the causation of such effects, whether the pill they recieve is real or not.

CROSSEYED
AND PAINLESS

In certain instances, the mind can override its programming and poison those it has been charged with protecting. This phenomenon is known as "voodoo death": where a healthy individual dies inexplicably following an ill omen, the breaking of a taboo, or a curse. While the phenomenon is almost nonexistent in technologically advanced societies where shamanism is not widely followed, there were instances of prisoners during the Korean War being subjected to Communist brainwashing, retiring to their beds, and dying within a few days, despite being in relatively good health. Fellow prisoners described the phenomenon as "give-up-itis."

RICHARD NIXON: LIBERAL MESSIAH

He was loathed by the liberals of his day, but contemporary members of the left would be clamoring to cast a vote for someone with these credentials.

ENVIRONMENTAL ISSUES

Understanding that the environments we live and work in are in need of considerable attention, Nixon started the EPA and OSHA, and instituted the Clean Air Act.

WORKING-CLASS HERO

Spurred on by the memory of losing two brothers as a youth, Nixon sought universal health care for Americans. His plan would have required employers to buy health insurance for their employees, and subsidized the employers who couldn't afford it. Unfortunately, the plan was shot down by Ted Kennedy, who later called it one of the biggest mistakes of his life. Nixon also backed a minimum guaranteed income for all Americans called the Family Assistance Program, which would have provided a payment to anyone who fell below a certain income level.

SO MUCH GRACIOUSNESS IN CUNNING

Like many liberals, he was no fan of conservative saint Ronald Reagan. In private, Nixon referred to the future president as a showy "know-nothing."

MY AIM IS TRUE

From 1970 to 1975, the annual budgets Nixon designed allocated more spending on human resource programs than on defense for the first time since World War II. And with the top tax rate at 70 percent during his presidency, that was not a negligible chunk of change.

ABOUT THE AUTHOR

Matthew Doucet is a writer and editor who lives in the foothills of New Hampshire's White Mountains. He spends his time trawling the internet for music and arguing with friends about things they don't know all that much about.

REFERENCES

A number of texts contributed to the composition of this book, but it would be nothing without the insight and inspiration provided by the following:

James Baldwin
The Price of the Ticket: Collected Nonfiction 1948–1985
St. Martin's Press, 1985

Anne Carson
Autobiography of Red
Knopf, 1998

Oriana Fallaci
Interview with History
Houghton Mifflin, 1977

William Finnegan
Barbarian Days: A Surfing Life
Penguin, 2015

Jane Jacobs
The Death and Life of Great American Cities
Random House, 1961

Julian Jaynes
The Origin of Consciousness in the Breakdown of the Bicameral Mind
Houghton Mifflin, 1976

Marshall McLuhan
The Gutenberg Galaxy
University of Toronto Press, 1962

John McPhee
Giving Good Weight
Macmillan, 1979

David Sheppard
On Some Faraway Beach: The Life and Times of Brian Eno
Orion, 2008

Tom Wolfe
The Electric Kool-Aid Acid Test
Farrar Strauss Giroux, 1968

ABOUT CIDER MILL PRESS
BOOK PUBLISHERS

Good ideas ripen with time. From seed to harvest,
Cider Mill Press brings fine reading, information,
and entertainment together between the covers of
its creatively crafted books. Our Cider Mill bears
fruit twice a year, publishing a new crop of titles
each spring and fall.

**BOOK
PUBLISHERS**

"Where Good Books Are Ready for Press"

Visit us online at
www.cidermillpress.com
or write to us at
PO Box 454
12 Spring St.
Kennebunkport, Maine 04046